Creative Doodle Designs

Valentine's Day

Helena Ann DeLuca

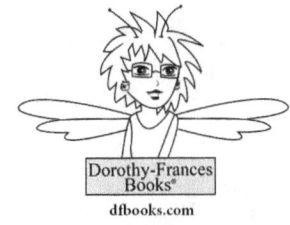

Dorothy-Frances
Books®

dfbooks.com

Creative Doodle Designs
Valentine's Day

Published by Dorothy-Frances Books®
First Edition; First Printing
www.dfbooks.com

ISBN-13: 978-0-9997911-1-0
ISBN:10: 0-9997911-1-7

25 Stress-Relieving Valentine Designs

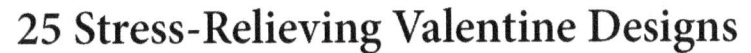

Enjoy coloring these Valentine's Day pages with accompanying inspirational quotes. Each coloring page is printed one-sided. Using a fine-point black pen or marker, add some of your own creative Doodle Design elements to the last 10 pages before coloring them. You can add doodles to any of the other pages, too!

Whatever your choice of coloring tool, whether it is crayons, markers, or colored pencils, I wish you hours of relaxation, stress relief, and creativity. — Helena

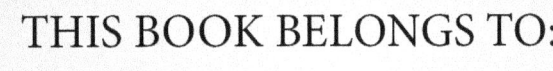

THIS BOOK BELONGS TO:

_____

When you arise in the morning, think of what a precious privilege it is to be alive—to breathe, to think, to enjoy, to love. *Marcus Aurelius*

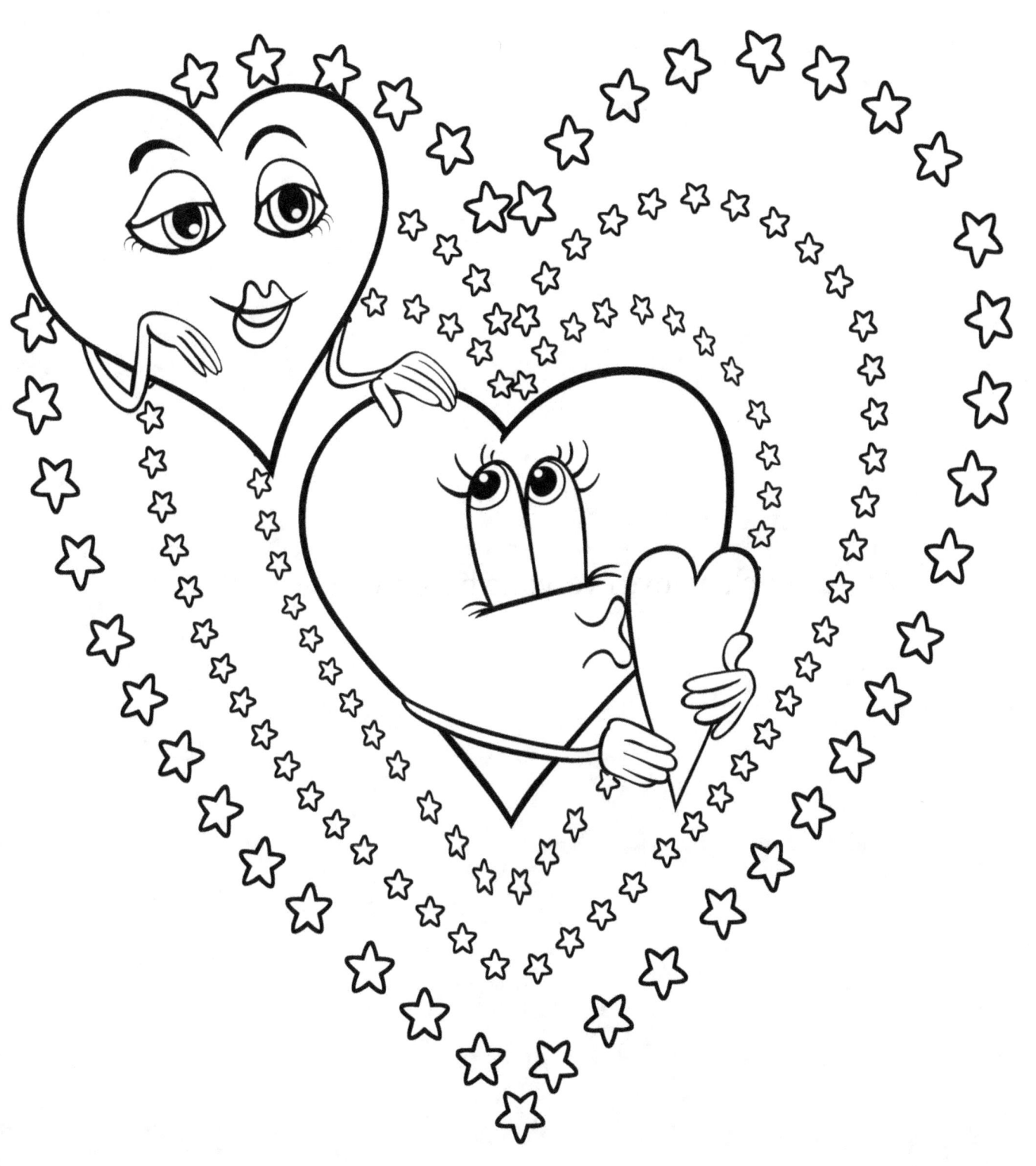

At the touch of love everyone becomes a poet. *Plato*

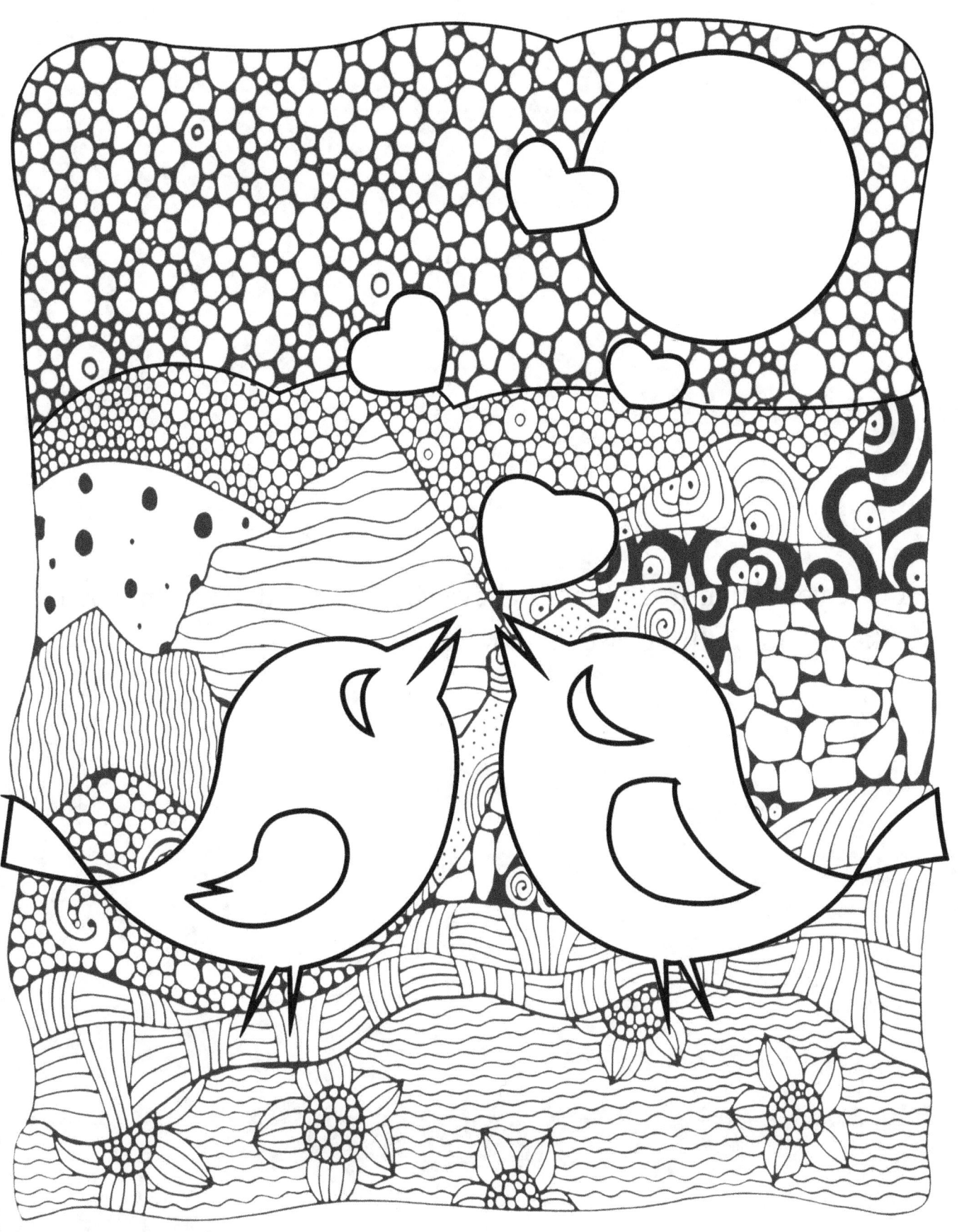

I love you the more in that I believe you had liked me for my own sake and for nothing else. *John Keats*

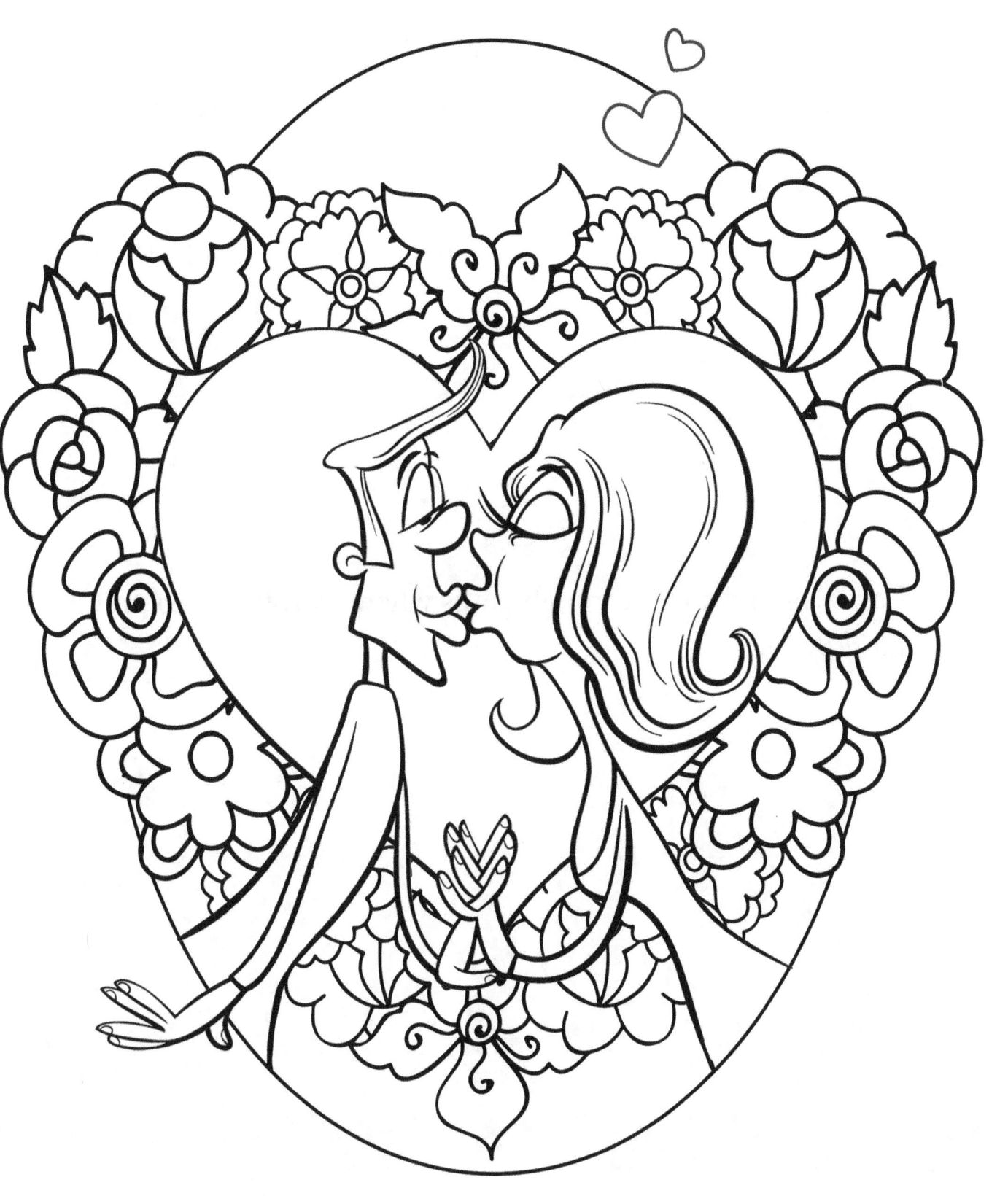

Love will find a way through paths where wolves fear to prey.
Lord Byron

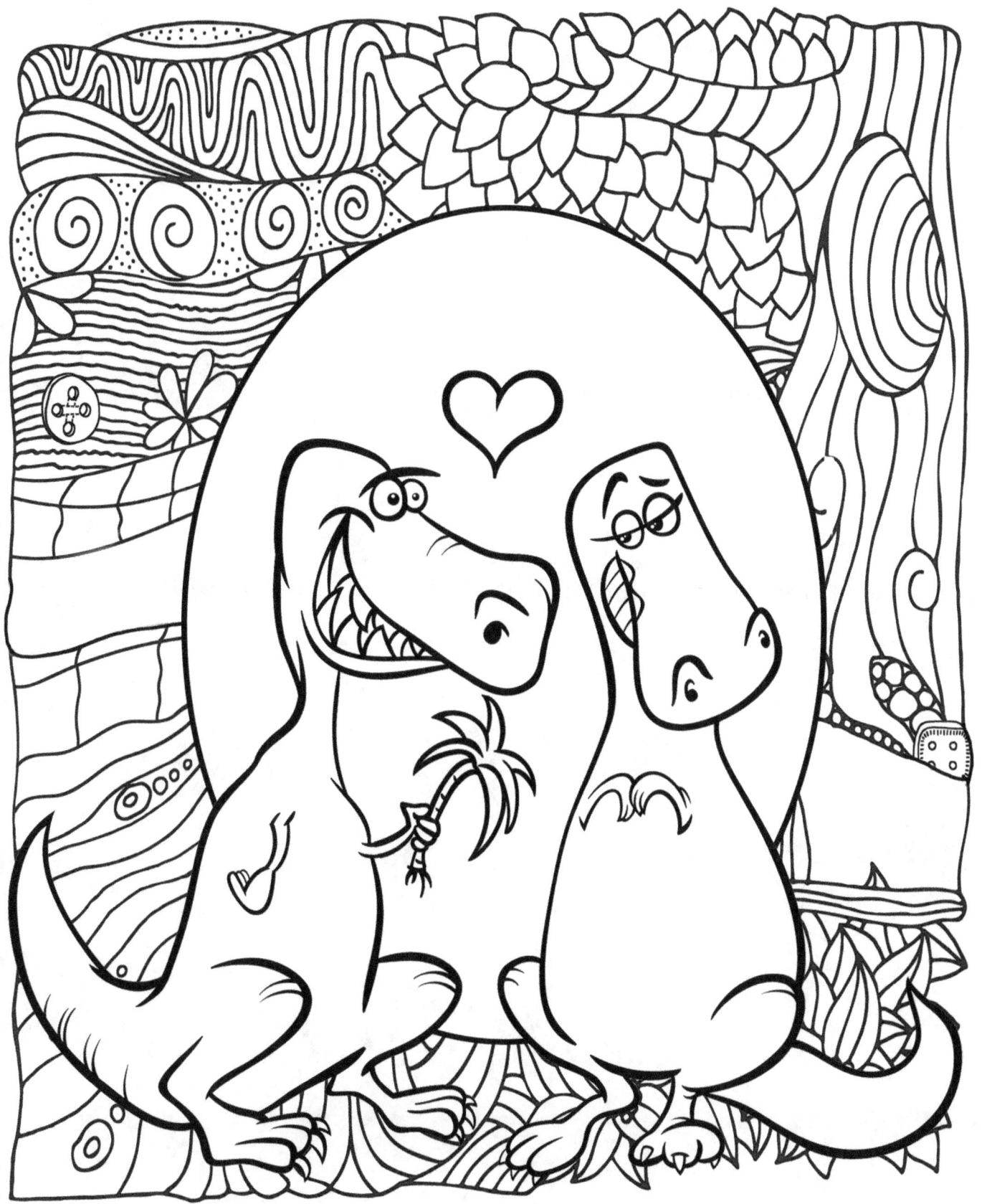

Love is space and time measured by the heart. *Marcel Proust*

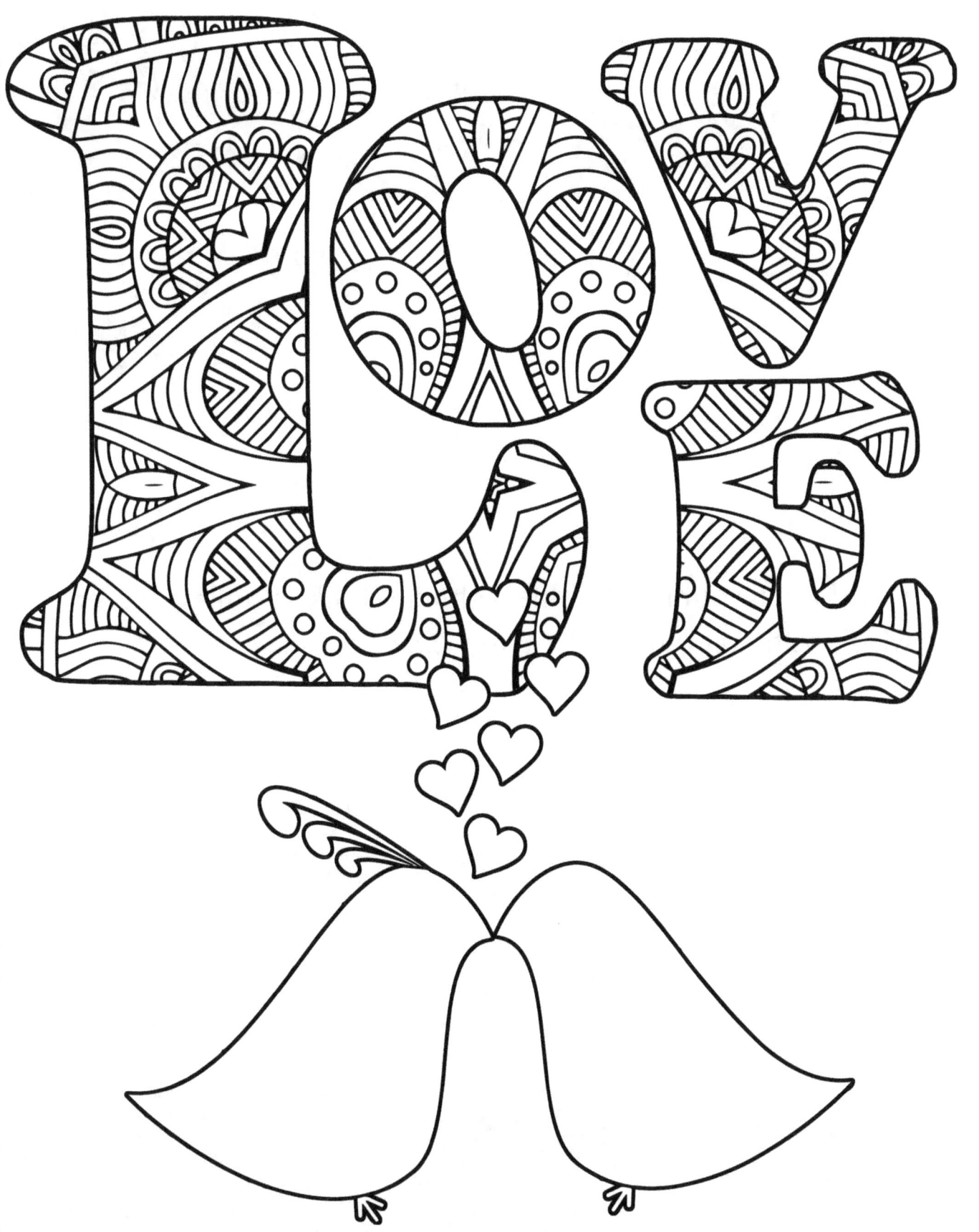

Keep love in your heart. A life without it is like a sunless garden when the flowers are dead. *Oscar Wilde*

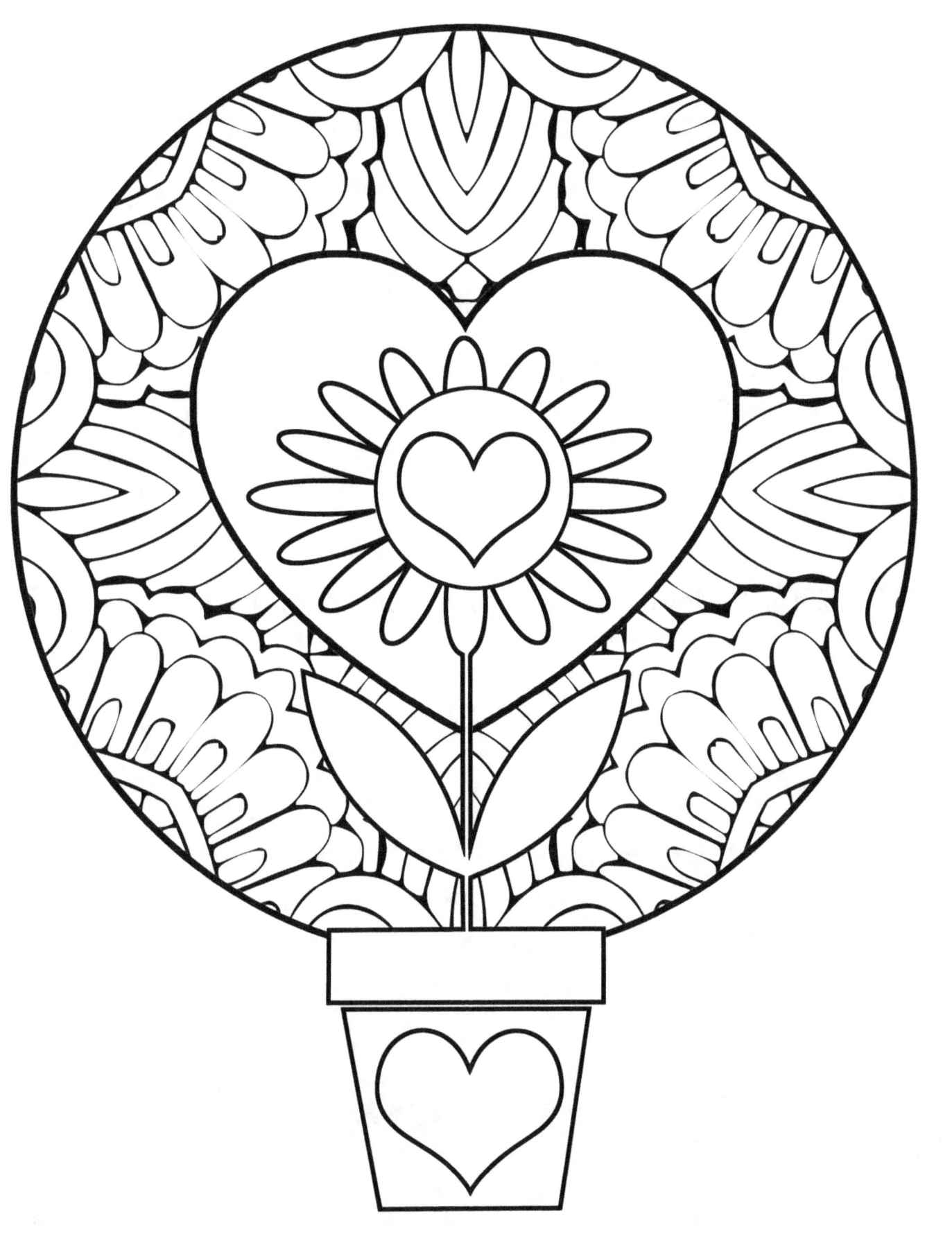

Life is the flower for which love is the honey. *Victor Hugo*

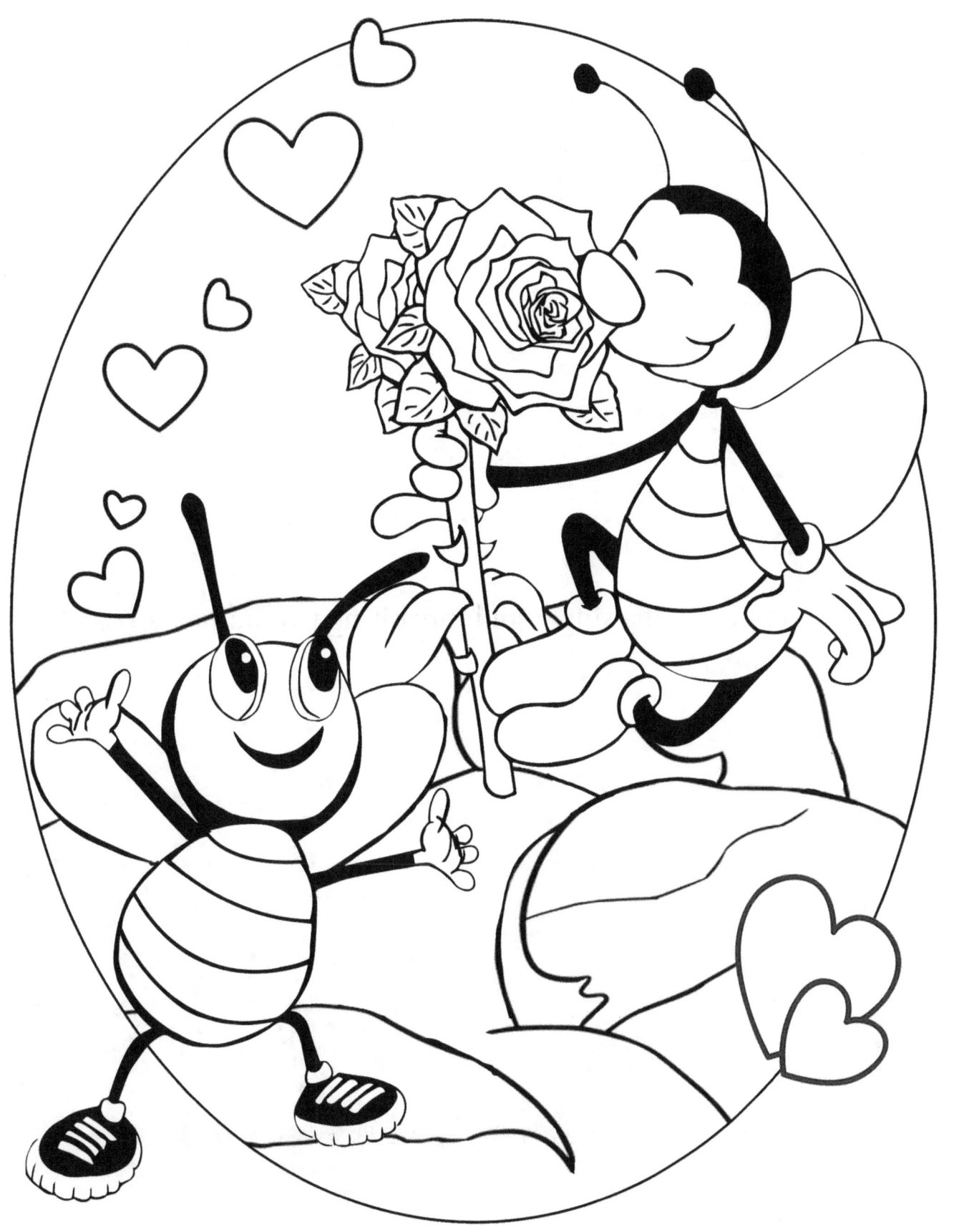

Love is composed of a single soul inhabiting two bodies. *Aristotle*

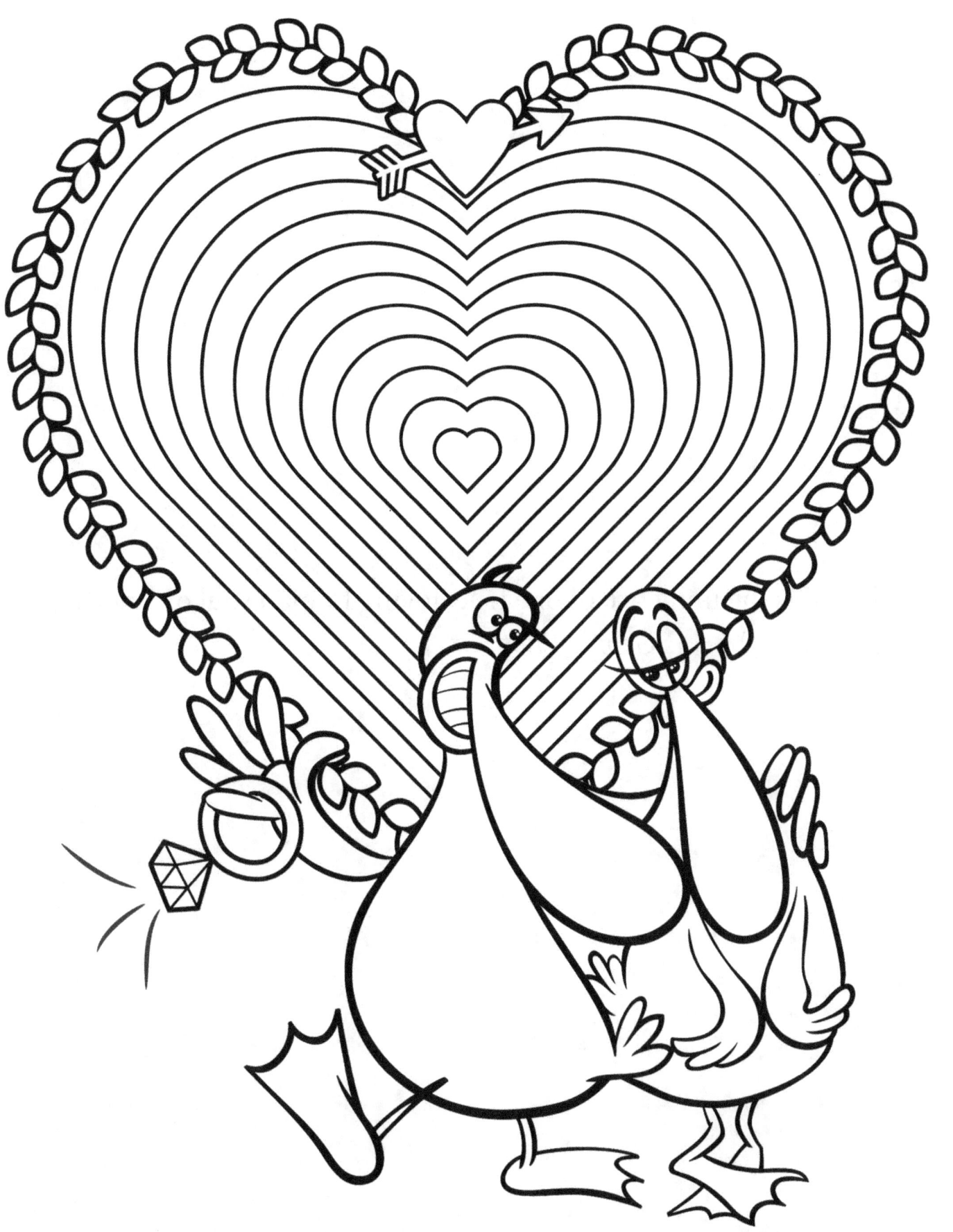

Blessed is the influence of one true, loving human soul on another.
Mary Ann Evan as George Eliot

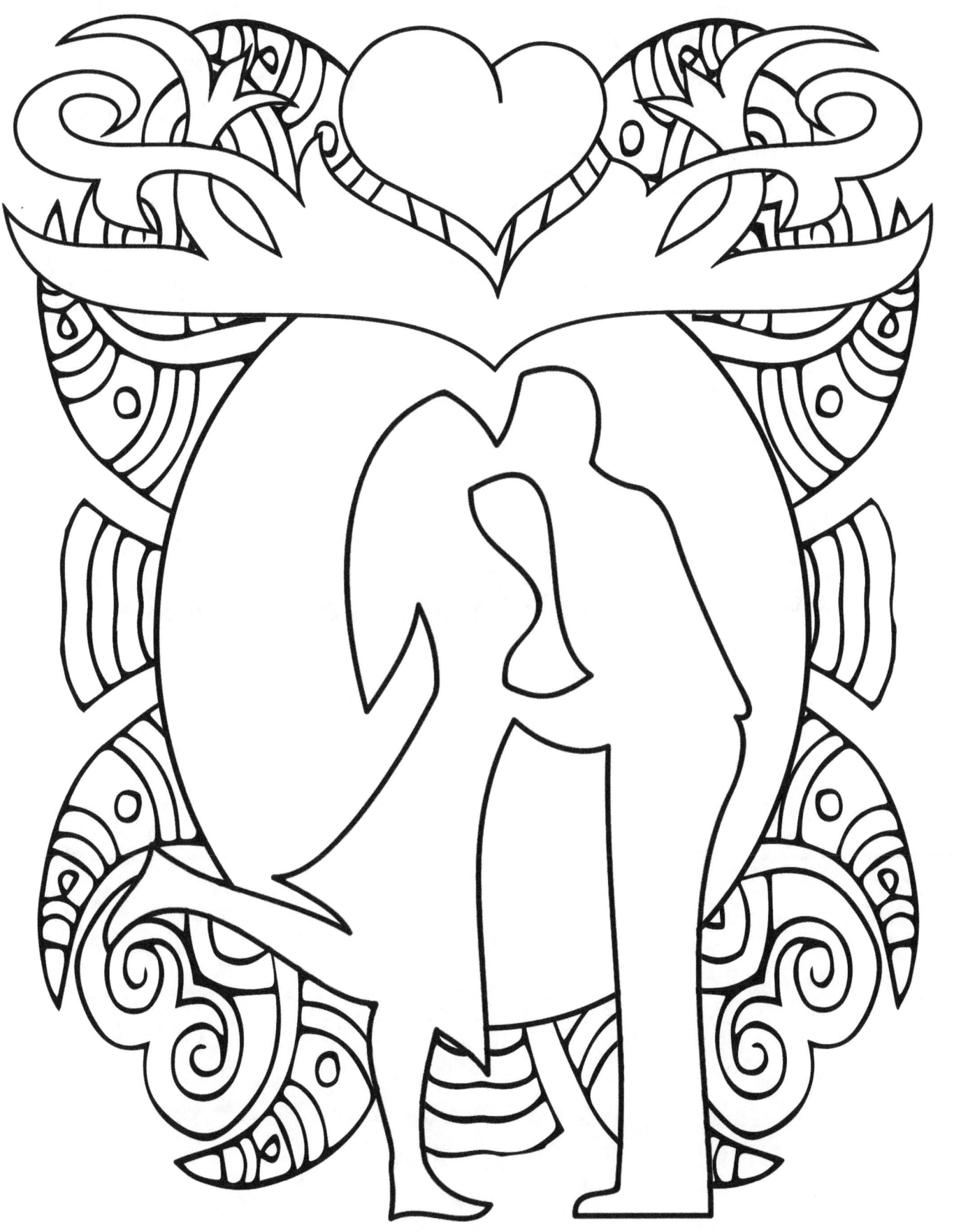

Wherever you go, go with all your heart. *Confucius*

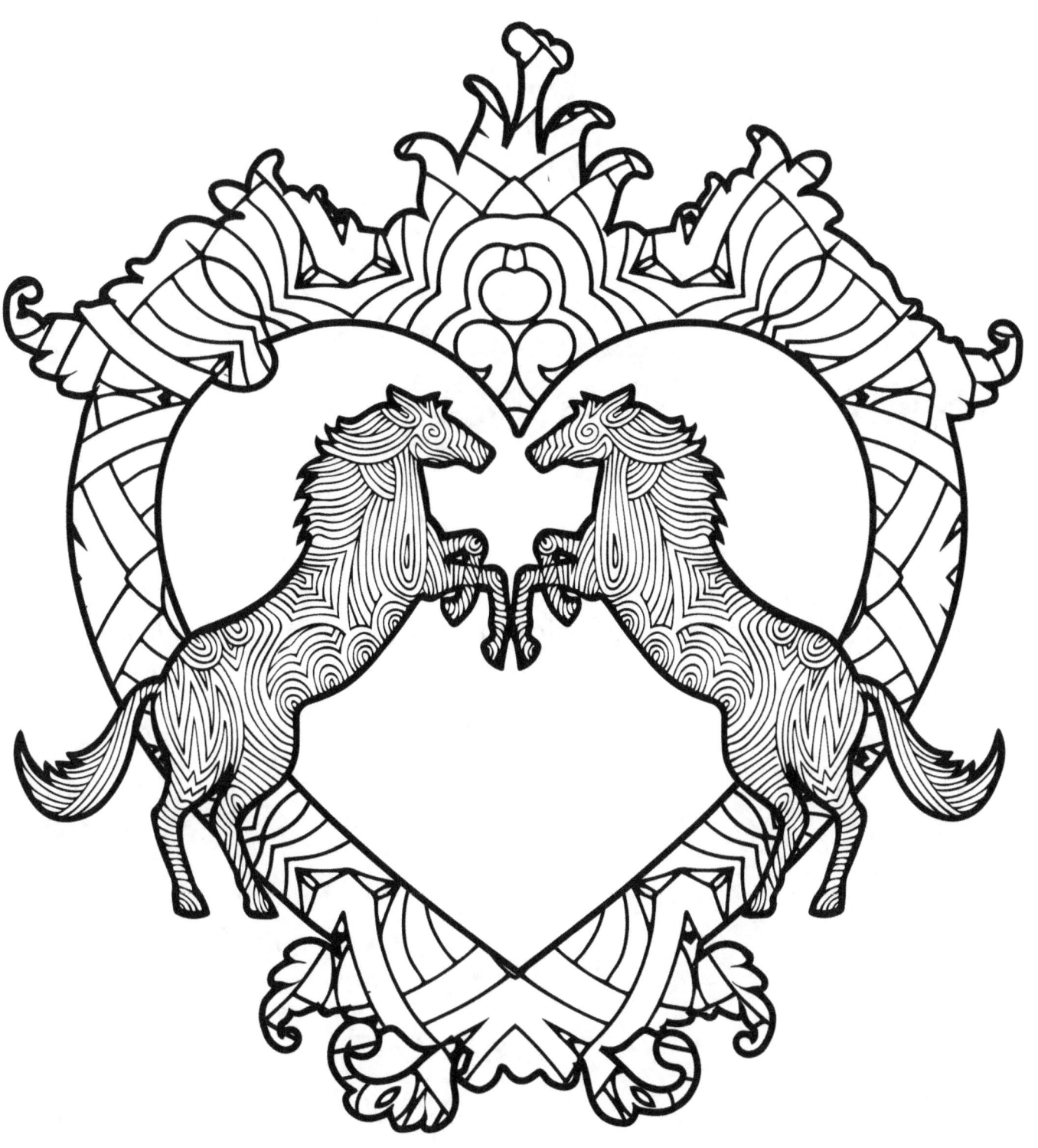

Unable are the loved to die, for love is immortality. *Emily Dickinson*

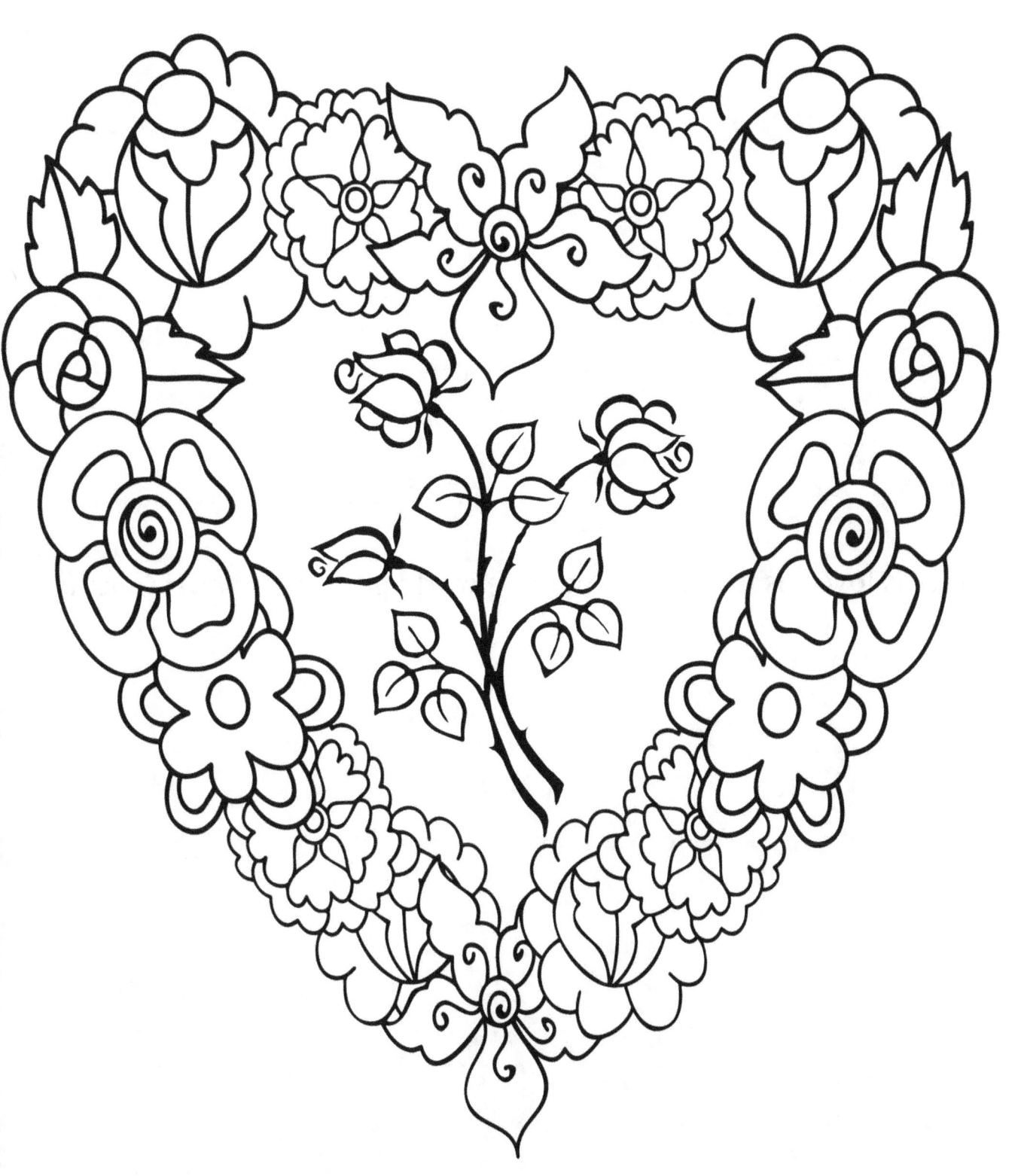

Oh, 'tis love, 'tis love that makes the world go round. *Lewis Carroll*

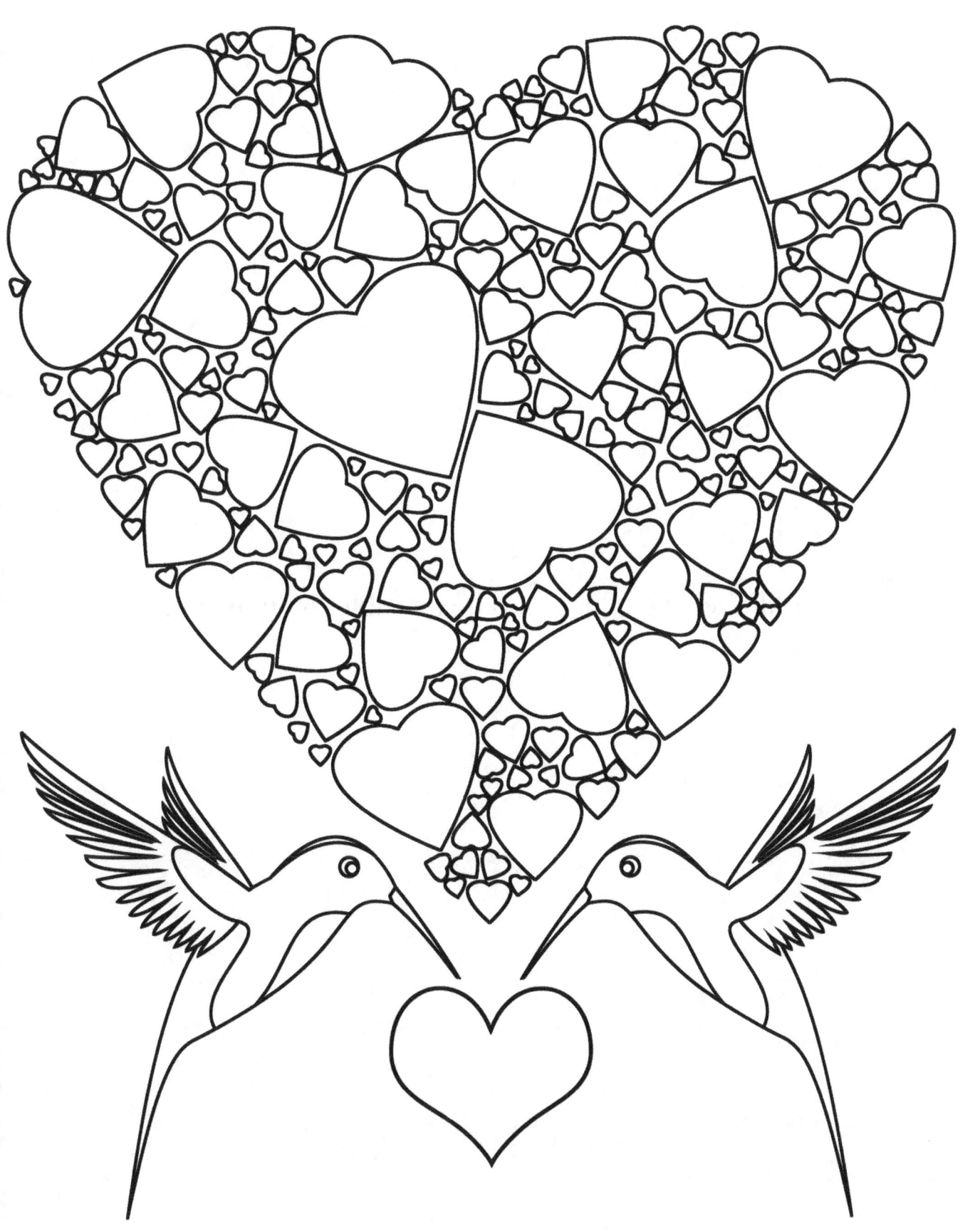

If you would be loved, love, and be loveable. *Benjamin Franklin*

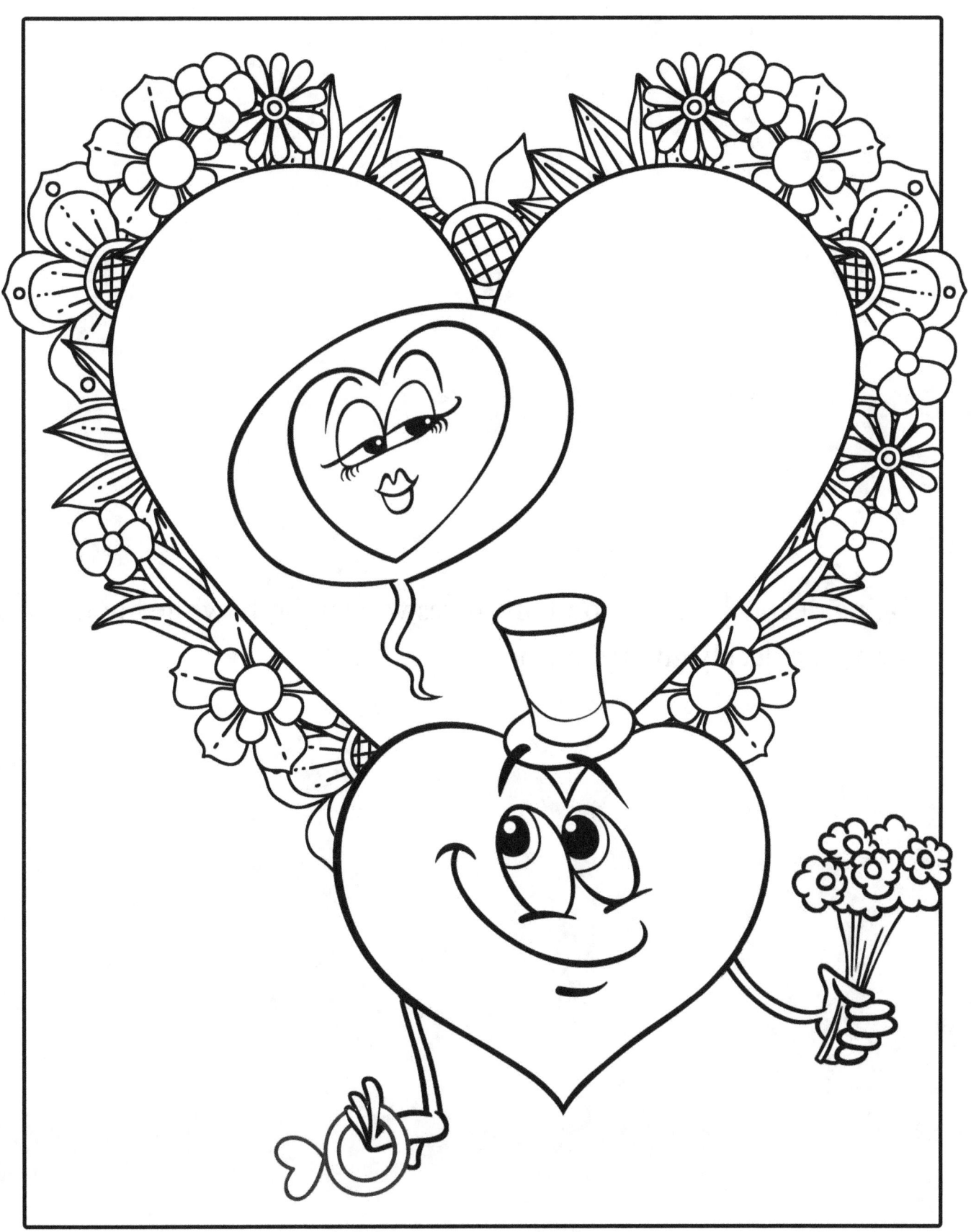

Being deeply loved by someone gives you strength, while loving someone deeply gives you courage. *Lao Tzu*

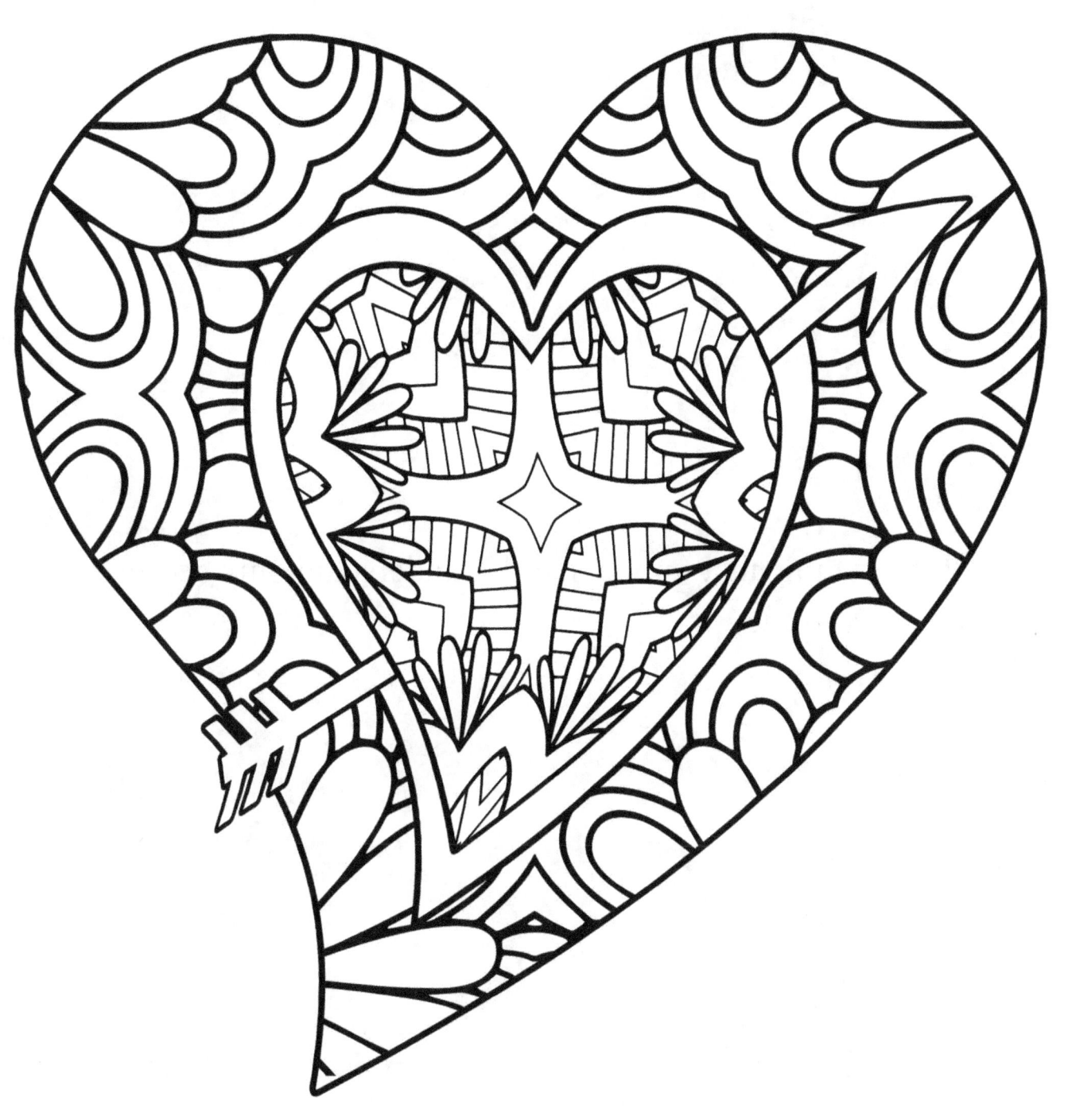

All, everything that I understand, I understand only because I love. *Leo Tolstoy*

Add some more butterflies in the center
of the heart before coloring!

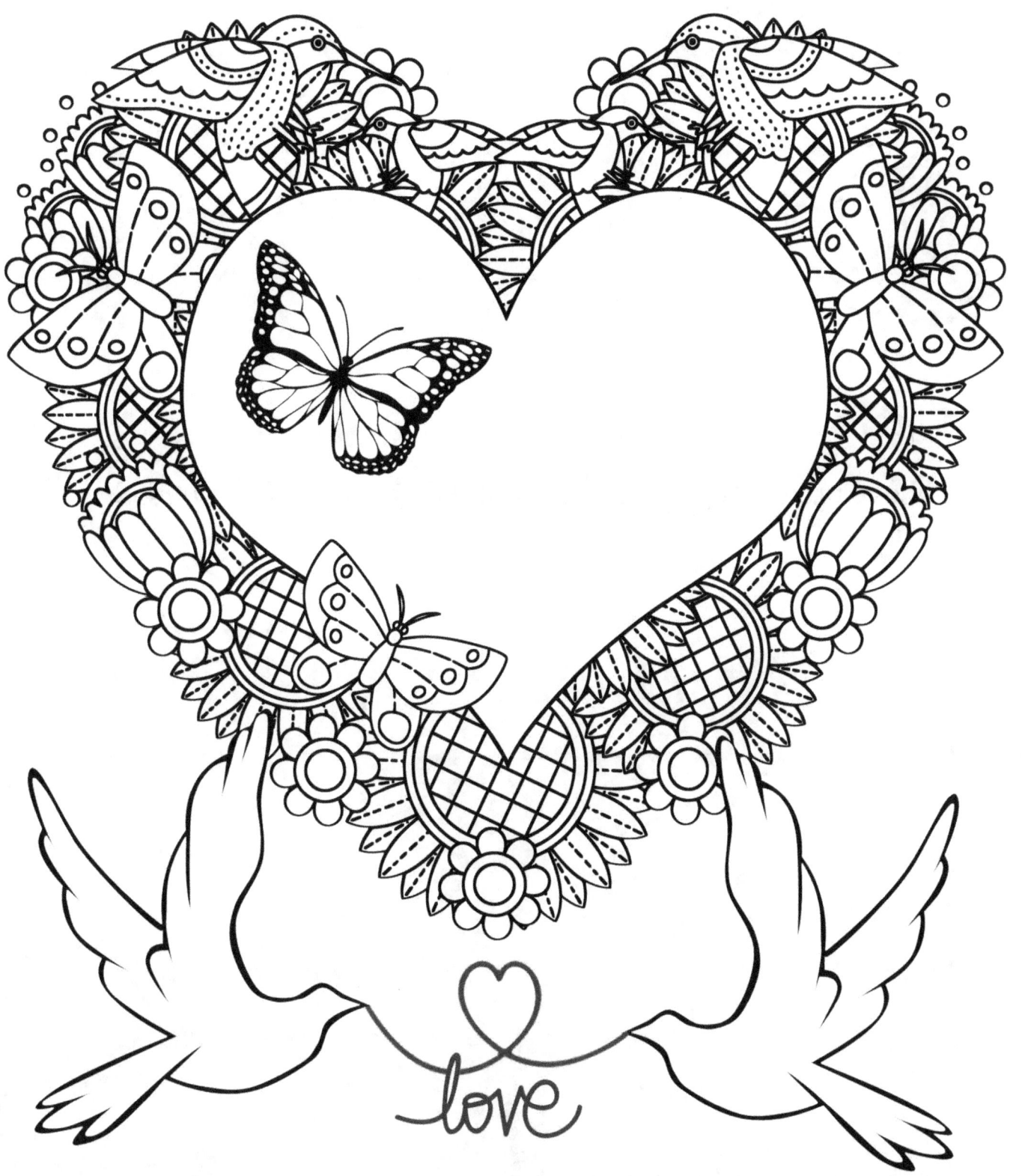

love

Love prefers twilight to daylight. *Oliver Wendell Holmes, Sr.*

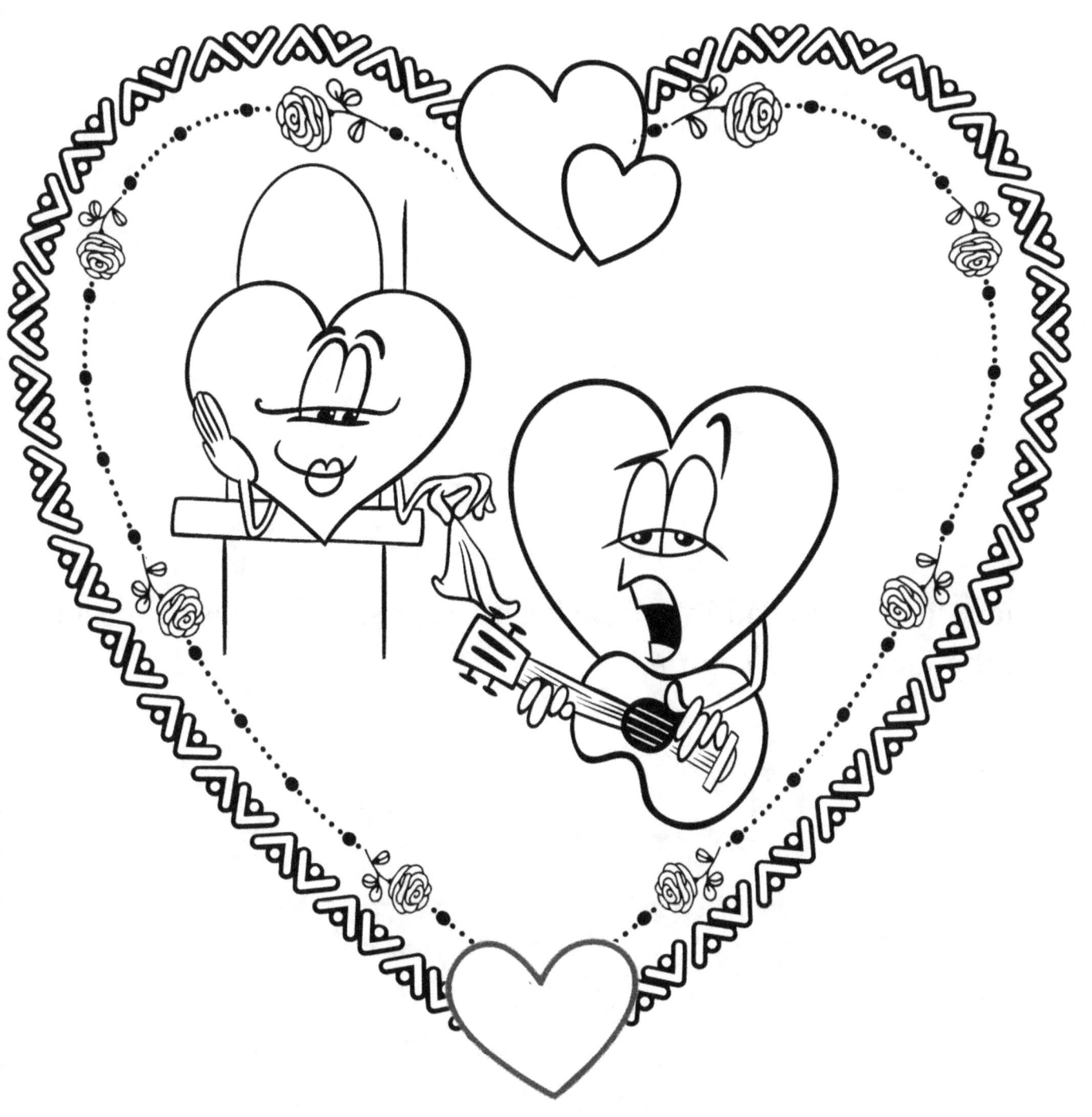

Doodle some background designs inside the heart!

Since love grows within you, so beauty grows. For love is the beauty of the soul. *Saint Augustine*

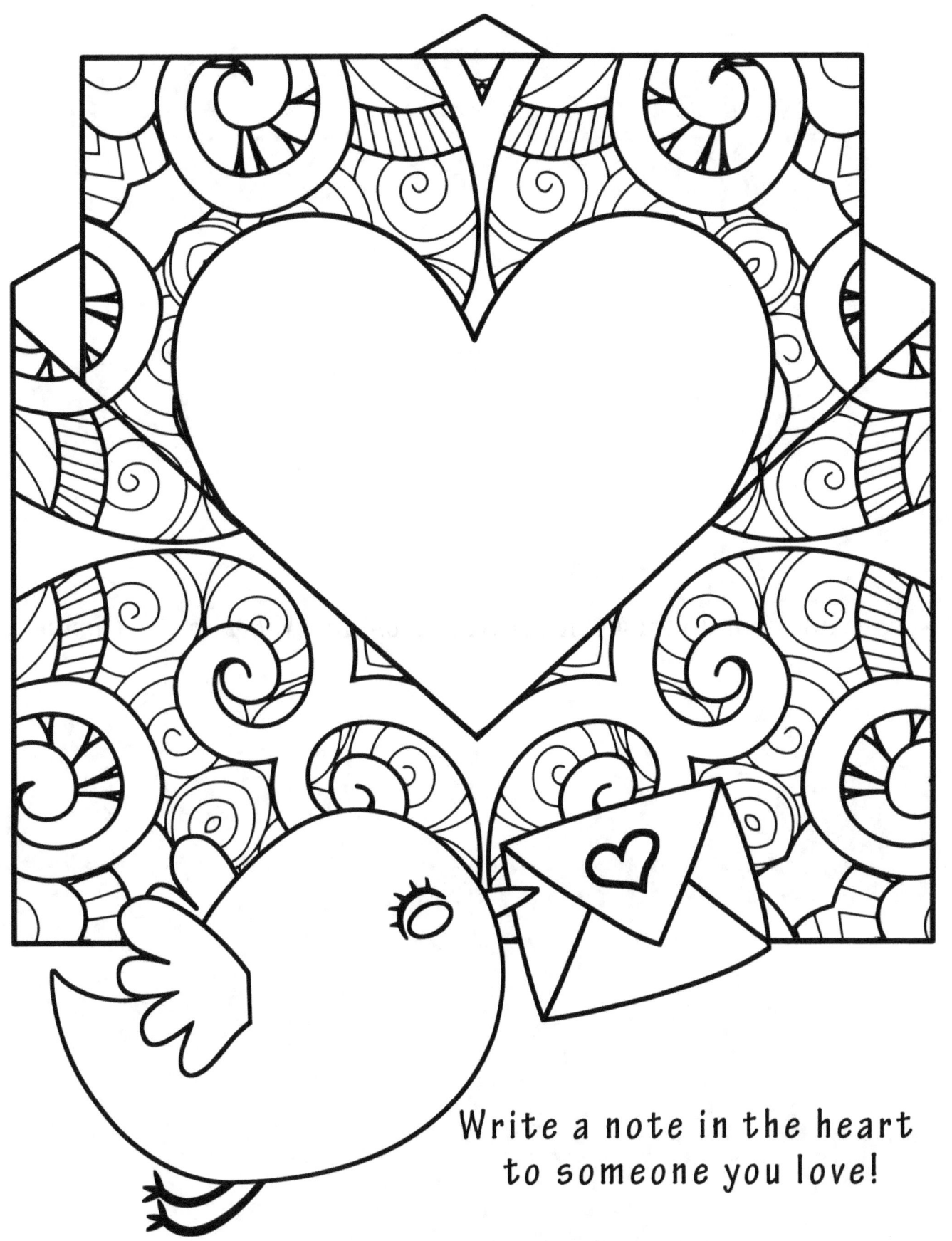

Write a note in the heart
to someone you love!

Love does not dominate; it cultivates. *Johann Wolfgang von Goethe*

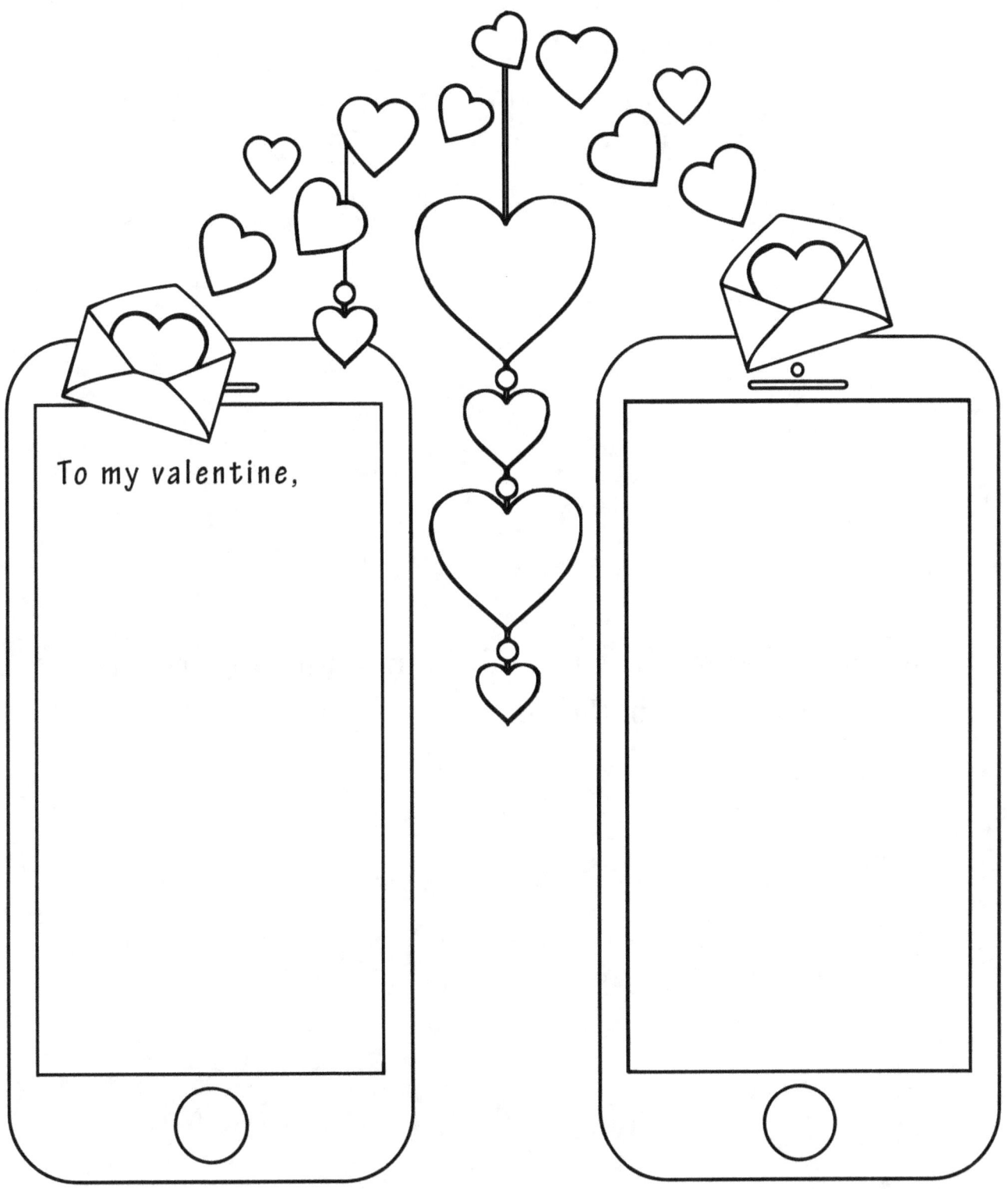

To my valentine,

Write a message to your valentine —and what message would you want him/her to send back?

You, yourself, as much as anybody in the entire universe, deserve your love and affection. *Buddha*

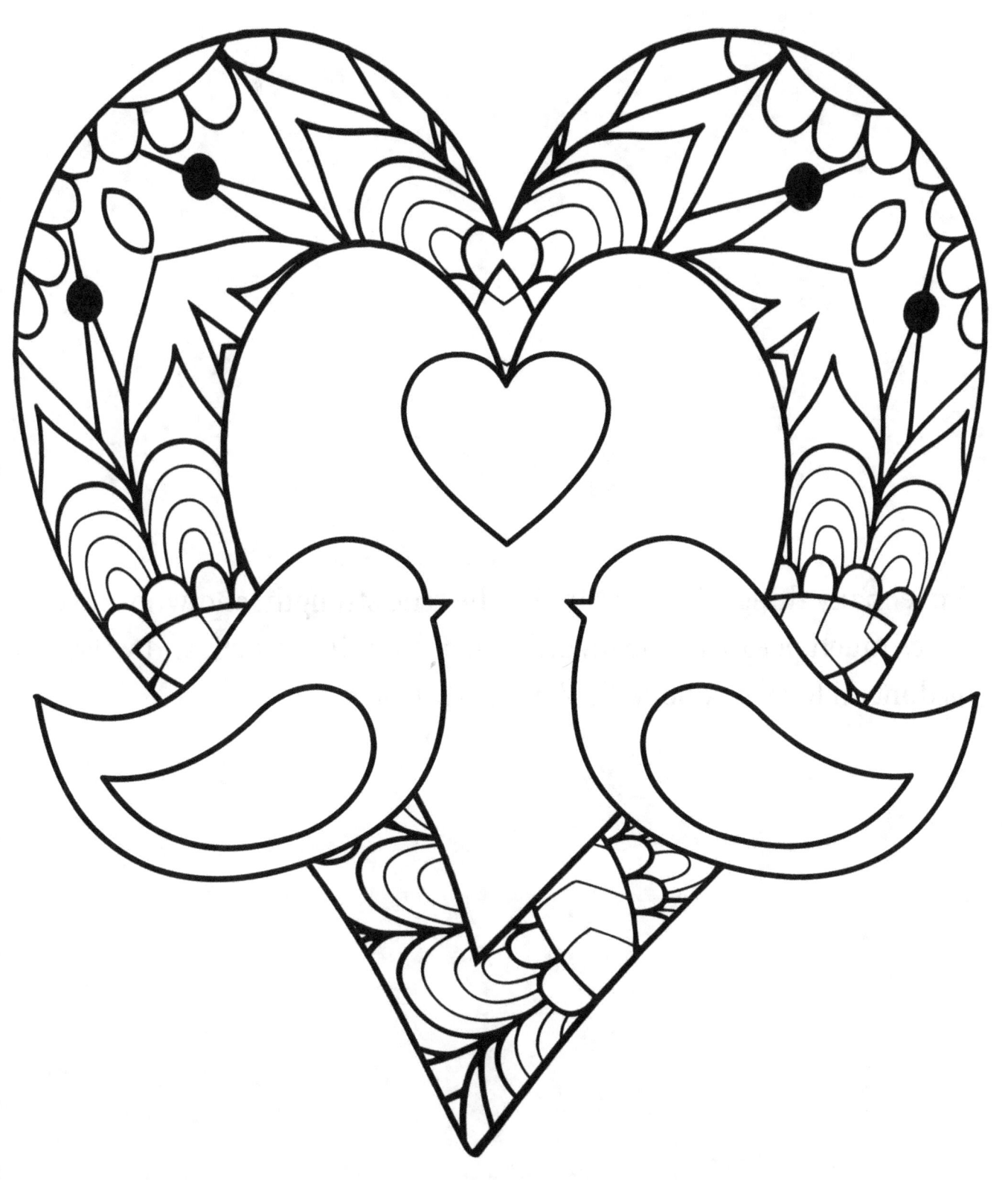

Doodle the lovebird's faces and feathers.

Love many things, for therein lies the true strength, and whosoever loves much performs much, and can accomplish much, and what is done in love is done well. *Vincent Van Gogh*

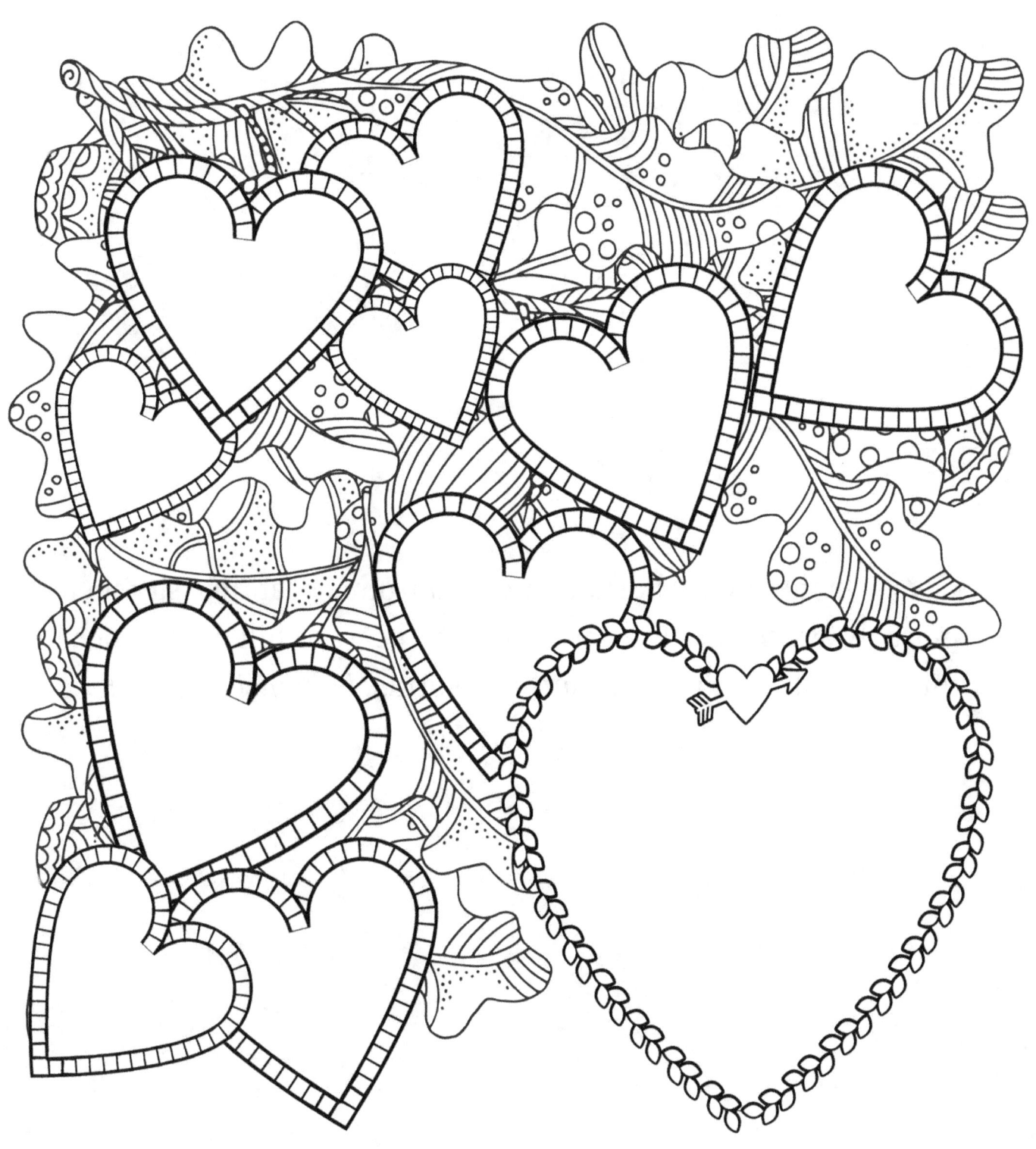

Doodle some designs inside the hearts!

Love, whether newly born, or aroused from a deathlike slumber, must always create sunshine, filling the heart so full of radiance, this it overflows upon the outward world. *Nathaniel Hawthorne*

Doodle designs inside the hearts
and then color them!

Accept the things to which fate binds you, and love the people with whom fate brings you together, but do so with all your heart.
Marcus Aurelius

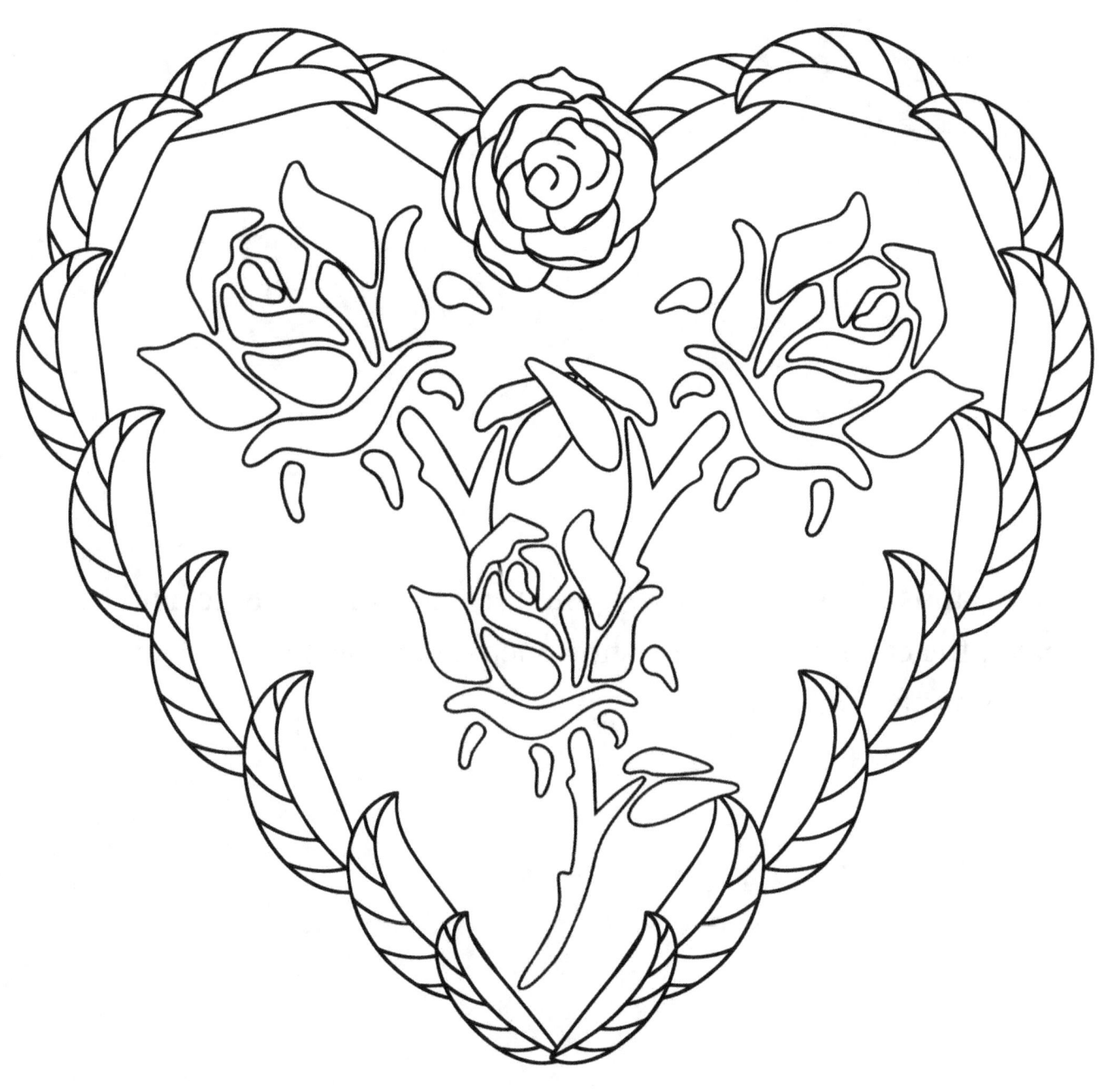

Add other doodle design elements
inside the heart before coloring it.

Thousands of candles can be lighted from a single candle, and the life of the candle will not be shortened. Happiness never decreases by being shared. *Buddha*

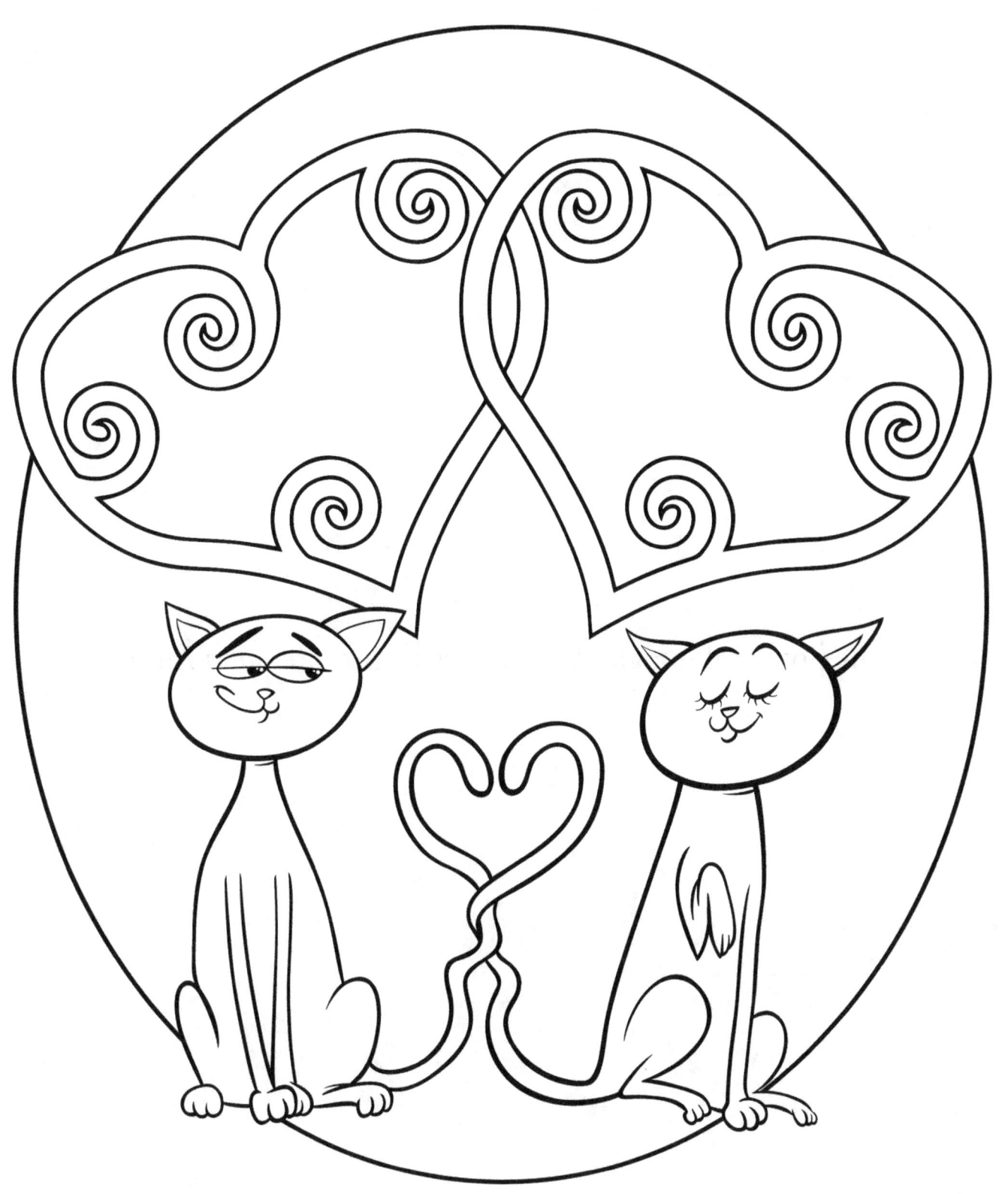

Doodle a background for the kitties . . .
and create a design in the hearts, too!

The power of imagination makes us infinite. *John Muir*

Doodle some details!

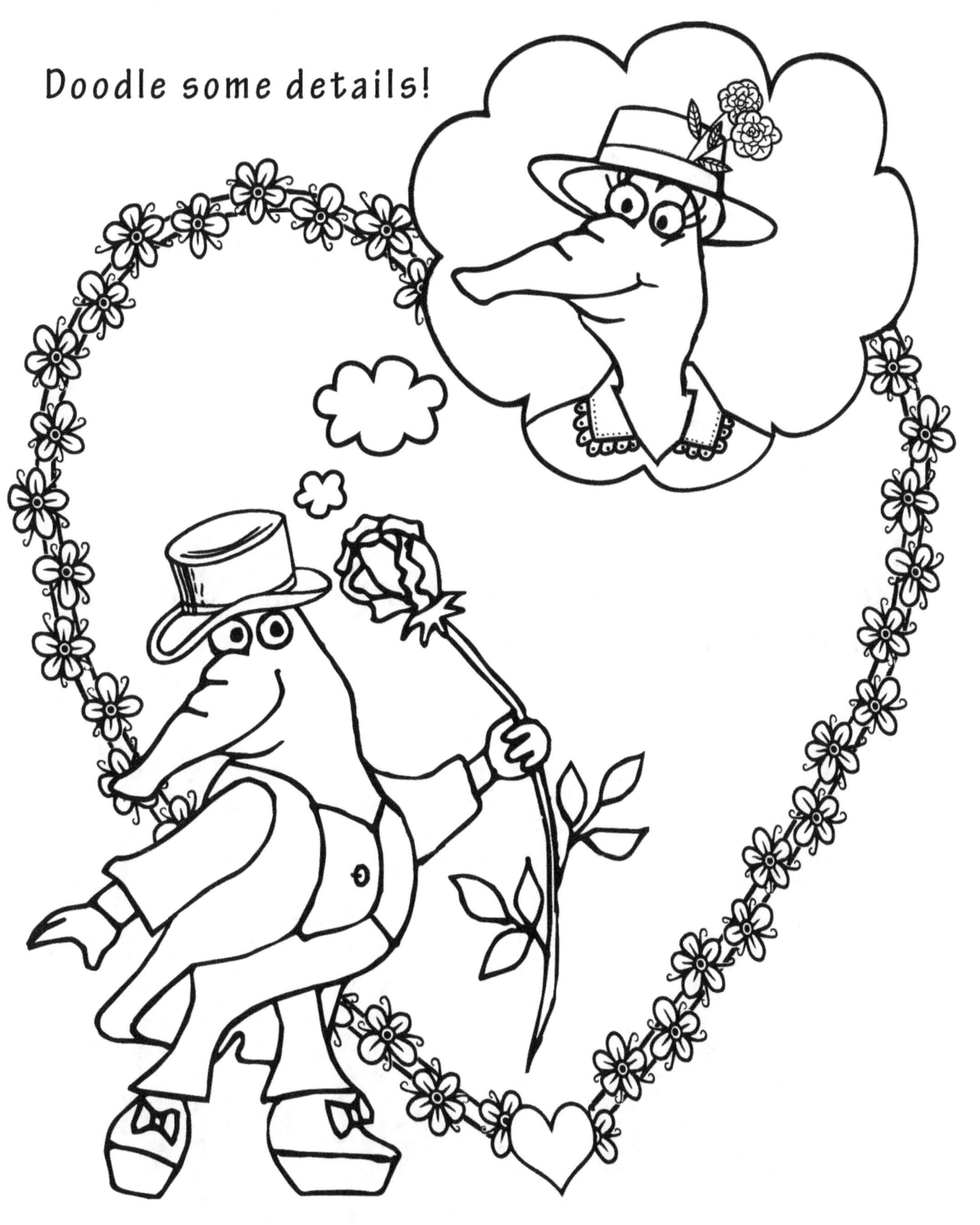

Keep your face always toward the sunshine—and shadows will fall behind you. *Walt Whitman*

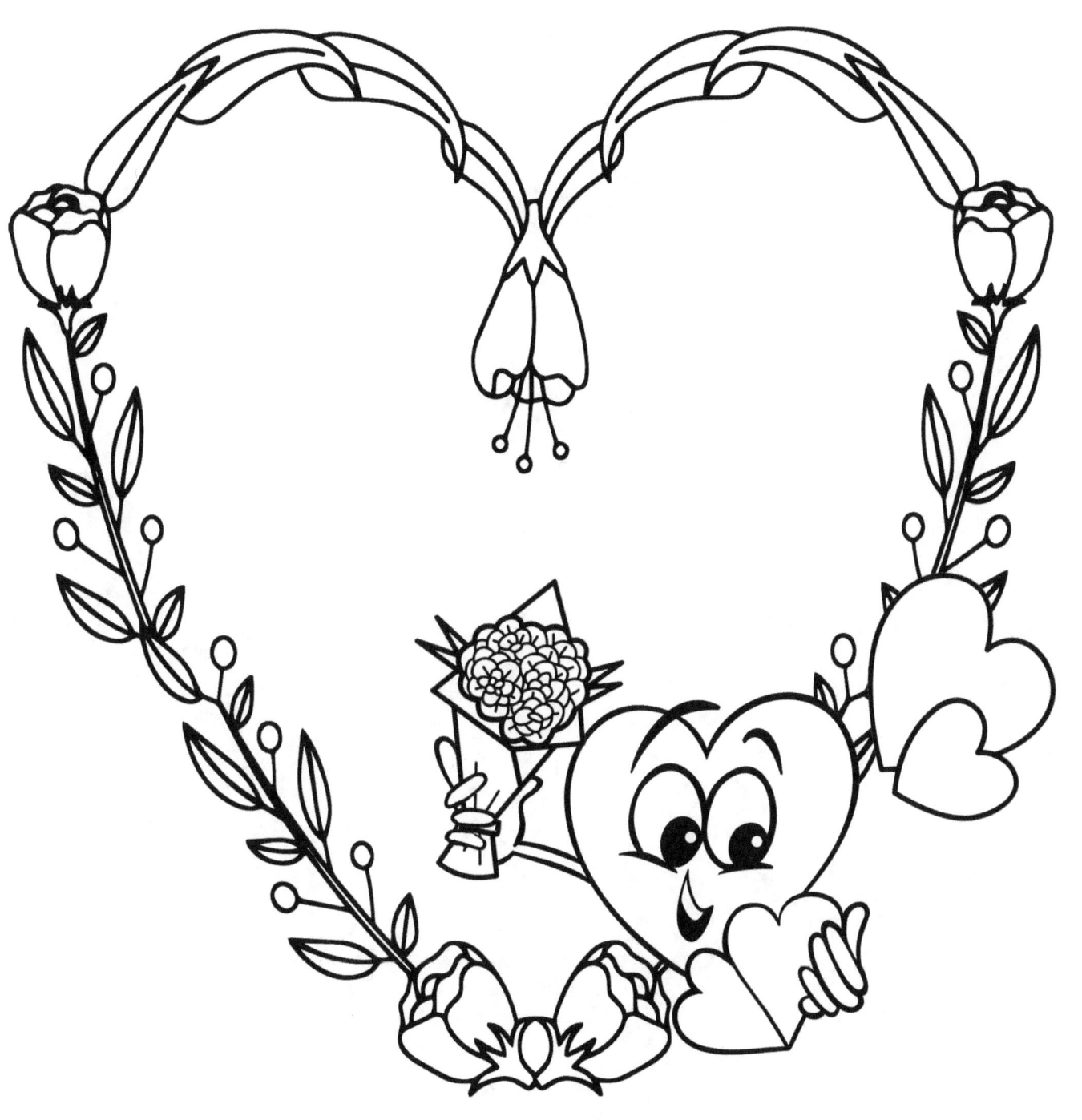

Doodle some more flowery designs
inside the heart?

The Creative Coloring® Series: Seasonal Coloring and Journal Books

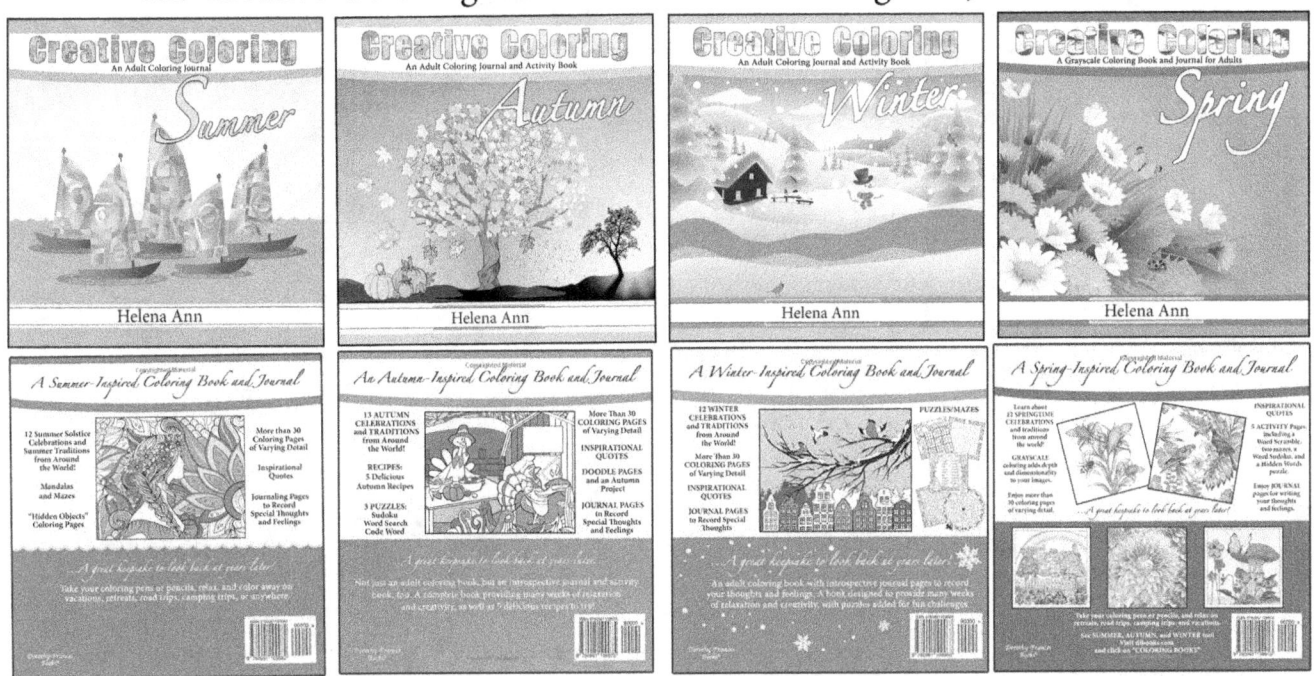

Other books also available on Amazon.com

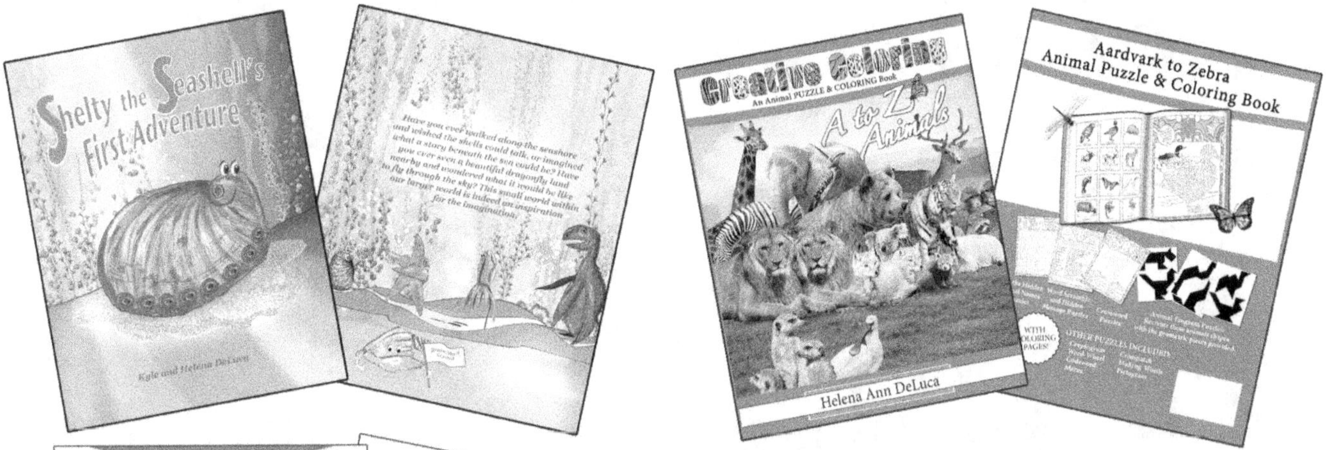

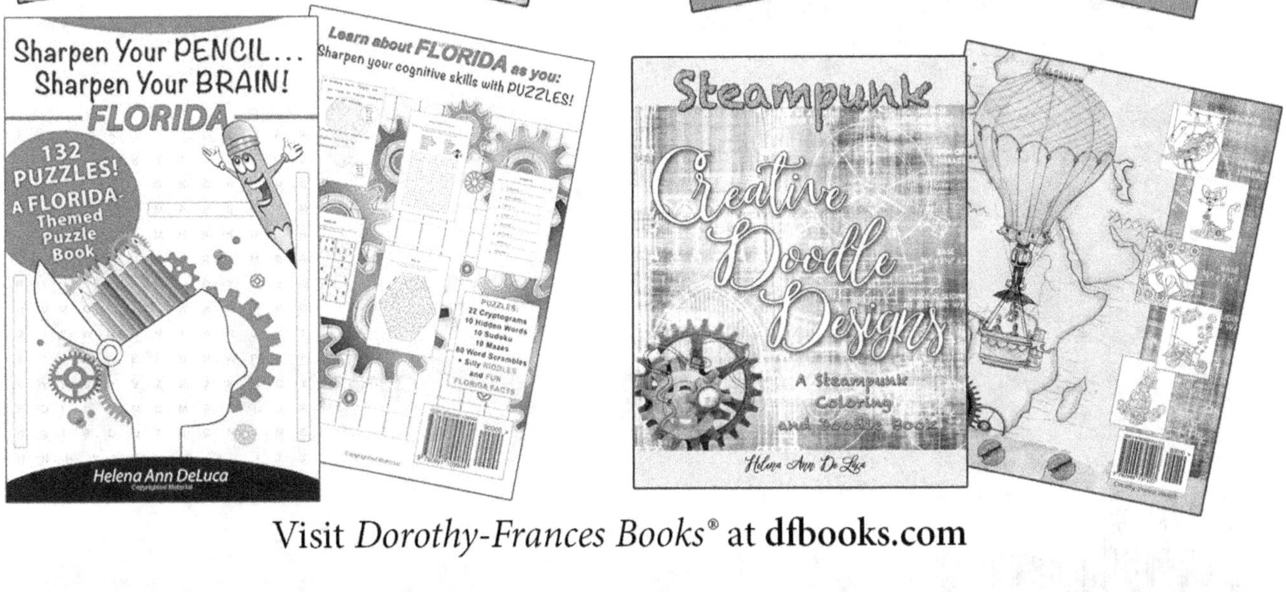

Visit *Dorothy-Frances Books*® at **dfbooks.com**